You Still Ghetto

You still Ghetto

You Know You're Still Ghetto If...

Bertice Berry, Ph.D.

 St. Martin's Griffin ♞ New York

ISBN 0-312-18236-8

First St. Martin's Griffin Edition: January 1998
10 9 8 7 6 5 4 3 2 1

Introduction

There has been a great deal of controversy and conversation surrounding the term *ghetto*. Morning radio programs and the Internet have been full of examples that much too often point to the underclass, and/or *those* inner-city individuals. In *Sckraight from the Ghetto: You Might Be Ghetto If . . .* we took an approach that brought the notion of ghetto back to where we all come from. We made it real for those who were in denial, the fact that ghetto has nothing to do with where you live, rather who you "be."

Rather than talk about "those" people (e.g., You know you're ghetto if your grandmother is under forty), we made the notion of ghetto much, much, much more inclusive (e.g., You know you're ghetto if there is a Maxwell House coffee can with bacon grease in the center of the burners of your stove).

While there were those who wanted to deny their roots—so to speak—(some of those folks were even named after characters in *Roots*), most people easily identified. Even Congresswoman Maxine Waters pointed out that she had just thrown out her coffee can with bacon grease, and she missed it.

We were pleased to hear from teachers who used the book in their classrooms to start conversations concerning where we all come from. Families shared the book at get-togethers, and had a good time reminiscing about their uncle Brother, the one who was both a drunk and a genius.

Overall, the response was tremendous. But you probably already realize that, especially since this is not the first ghetto book that you've borrowed.

We were somewhat surprised, however, by those well-meaning folks who refused to see themselves, and felt it necessary to defend others who do, in fact, carry a purse with their jogging suit, can remember having a bike with one pedal and a steering wheel, or who have a brother named Brother. These were those proud folks who choose to view ghetto as demeaning. They see it as a term that refers to *those poor people over there*, and not to themselves.

I was surprised by the reaction of those "special" book reviewers. You know, the ones who draw their conclusions based on the title of the book, or on what others had to say—and I really mean *those*.

The biggest surprise, however, came from those who never ever want to be reminded of where they're from. They are in denial and would like to stay that way. They are proud to be the first black who did whatever it is that they have done, and are fighting desperately to hold on to that title. They not only have no intention of sending the ladder back down—they intend to burn it. They refuse to recognize that being the first black in this day and age is a reflection of the time and not of their individuality. We are where we are because of those ancestors who made it possible for us to be here. Yes, they scratched and survived, some even shucked and jived, but they are the reason that we are where we are.

As ghetto as some of their techniques were, they helped us to get over. The problem we have now is that we don't know which of these things we can let go of (e.g., the notion of good and bad hair), and which we should hold on to (e.g., finding someone to scratch your scalp on your front porch).

This leads me to the purpose of writing this book. It is an attempt to hasten the healing process for those of us who recognize, "Yeah, we ghetto, and we would like to stop talking back to the movie screen, but would like to remember the feeling we had when we did it." In short, it's about recalling a time when we were much more of a community, even though we didn't have the proverbial pot to piss in, or the window to throw it out. In *You Still Ghetto*, we will remember those times and determine which we should maintain and which of those we should throw out with the bathwater. Before we proceed, let's review a few necessary points.

Ghetto Review

Ghetto is not about where you live. It's about where you're coming from. Ghetto has nothing to do with poverty. It is a state of mind. Mine and yours.

The original connotation of the word *ghetto* had to do with an area comprised primarily of one ethnic or racial group, originating with Jewish ghettos. However, practically all American neighborhoods are divided in this fashion. If, then, we were to rely solely on Webster's definition then everyone—including Webster—is ghetto. This is not too far from the truth. However, for the purposes of this book, we need to be a tad more specific.

At its very core, ghetto has to do with getting by and making it against the odds. It deals with using every resource available and those that are on layaway, to make ends meet. Sometimes the ends make no sense at all. But when you are playing the game of life, and no one has bothered to deal you in, you do whatever is necessary.

Many of our ghetto traits have been handed down from generation to generation, without anyone ever stopping to question why they exist. For example, eating chitterlings and greens cooked in fatback. This is not exclusive to poor people or inner-city folks. It is something we continue to do because we have learned that it is good.

Who Is Ghetto

It was explained in *Sckraight from the Ghetto* that you don't have to be poor or old to be ghetto. Never has there been a better example than the very wealthy and the very young Tiger Woods, the Masters golf champ. Mr. Woods proclaimed that he was not African-American; rather, he prefers to see himself as *cablasian* (Caucasian, black, and Asian). Only a ghettoite—correction: only a black ghettoite—could even come up with a word like *cablasian*.

Where Do Ghettoites Dwell?

Just look around you and then look in the mirror. Wherever there is project heat, there is a ghettoite. Now before you go thinking that you have to go to the projects to find project heat, let me point out that if you go to practically any of the so-called luxury apartments in any northern city, you'll find that in the wintertime those windows are opened wider than are the ones in Cabrini Green.

Ghetto Test

In *Sckraight from the Ghetto*, we helped individuals determine whether or not they were in fact ghetto. We proved beyond the shadow of the Shadow that basically everybody was to some degree or another ghetto.

We also pointed out ways that one could be anti-ghetto, and therefore anti-community (e.g., If you go to black clubs to pick up white women. . . . If you have more shoes than you have books, etc.). The test in *You Still Ghetto* will be to determine which of these items you should let go of, and which of them you should keep. Unfortunately, as we assimilate more and more into the dominant culture, we not only try to forget where we have come from, we also leave behind the tools and more importantly, the people who helped us get to wherever it is that we think we are. One simply needs to look at O.J. Simpson to realize that you better not never forget who you are and where you're from.

The book is also divided by topics. It contains topics that appeared in *Sckraight from the Ghetto*, and I have also included topics that many of you rather loudly pointed out that I had forgotten. Things like Ghetto Superstitions, Ghetto Sayings, and Ghetto Pickup Lines. For my West Indian friends who said, "I know I'm not ghetto 'cause I'm from Jamaica, but we do this too," I've included a special section just for you (West Indian Ghetto). Enough about what the book is about. You got it, and by now you know that You Still Ghetto. So go on and read and let the healing continue.

YOu KnOw yOu're Still Ghetto If...

1. You have all of the *Ebony*s ever printed.

2. You use a matchbook or other items to level your furniture.

3. No one is allowed in the living room.

4. You ever had plastic kitchen curtains.

5. You have candles, but you never light them and they're dusty.

6. Your walls smell like everything you've ever cooked.

7. You have more dead bugs in your light fixtures than on a fly strip.

8. The house is filled with fake flowers.

Ghetto Home
And Gardens

YOu KnOw YOu're Still Ghetto If...

9. You have a fake fireplace with fake logs.

10. You had an aluminum Christmas tree with a color wheel.

11. You still eat Jiffy Pop popcorn.

12. Your coffee table has cigarette burns.

2

13. None of your furniture matches, but you call it a set.

14. Your sofa has a dip in it.

15. Your baseboards are a different color than the walls, but the difference isn't the paint.

16. You have so many stuffed animals on your bed that no one can sleep there.

17. You never use your dining room.

Ghetto Home And Gardens

18.
The dining room table is set just for decoration.

YOu KNOw yOu're Still Ghetto If...

19. You need a map to get around your furniture.

20. You brag about having silver but never polish it.

21. You feel you have to clean up before the housekeeper comes.

22. Your floor is sticky.

23. Your trash bag is on your refrigerator door.

24. You eat from a TV tray.

25. You still have TV trays.

26. Your doorknobs are always dirty.

27. You have carpet on your porch.

28. There is a saint in your front yard.

4

Ghetto Home And Gardens

YOu KnOw yOu're Still Ghetto If...

29. You have a fountain as big as your front yard.

30. You have frosted diamond mirrors on your living room wall.

31. There are nails in your walls with nothing hanging on them.

32. You have cigarette burns in your leather furniture.

33. All your coffee cups are stained.

34. Your front porch is carpeted but not enclosed.

35. The pattern in your wallpaper doesn't line up.

36. You started painting your house, but never finished, and just left it that way.

37. Your lamp shades have fringe around the bottom.

Ghetto Home And Gardens

yOu kNOw yOu're Still Ghetto If...

38. You try to decorate your house like the ones in *Dynasty*.

39. The outsides of your windows have never been cleaned.

40. You clean your windows with vinegar and newspaper.

41. You have picture of your family members taped to your walls.

42. Your cabinet and closet doors are always open.

43. The mice come out when company comes.

44. You hang all of your hats on nails.

45. The bottoms of your pots are black from burning.

Ghetto Home And Gardens

46. The handles of your spatulas are all burned.

You Know You're Still Ghetto If...

47. Your wooden spoons are so worn down that they look like knives.

48. None of your silverware is silver.

49. None of your dish set match.

50. All of your dishes are chipped.

51. Your dishrags are really rags.

52. The floorboards under your sink are warped.

53. You know what time your roaches come out.

54. You don't have a garbage disposal but you act like you do.

55. Your dirty stove has more food in it than your refrigerator.

Ghetto Home And Gardens

YOu KnOW yOu're Still Ghetto If...

56. You had one of those TV color screens for a black-and-white TV. (You can remember it, but you've never told your children about it.)

57. You have to bang on your TV to get a decent picture.

58. You can't watch TV because you lost the remote.

59. Your carpet has a clear path from the chair in front of the television to the refrigerator.

60. The top of your refrigerator is so dirty that your cereal boxes get stuck.

61. Your light switch is missing its plate cover.

62. The clock on your VCR is always blinking.

63. Your VCR belongs in a museum.

YOu KnOw yOu're Still Ghetto If...

64. Your television is larger than your sofa.

65. Your television/stereo system requires five remote controls.

66. You switch batteries from one remote control to another.

67. All of the cords to the electrical appliances and light fixtures are painted the same color as the walls.

11

68. You play your television like it's a stereo.

69. Your television is always on and no one's home.

70. Your appliances are always repaired by your Uncle Booky.

71. You're a whiz at changing electrical fuses.

Ghetto-Lectronics

YOu KnOw yOu're StiII Ghetto If...

72. You don't mind when there is a power outage.

73. You refuse to talk on the phone during a storm.

12

YOu KnOW yOu're Still Ghetto If...

74. You walk on the back of your shoes.

75. You wear your underwear as outerwear.

76. You wear Tommy Hilfiger.

77. You have alligator shoes in all the primary colors and suits to match.

78. You and your man wear matching outfits.

79. None of your socks match.

80. You have a hat to match every outfit.

81. You have a baseball hat collection.

82. You still wear Candies.

83. You have more clothes in your closet that don't fit than those that do.

YOu KNOw yOu're Still Ghetto If...

84. You wear sunglasses indoors.

85. You have a pair of sunglasses to match every outfit.

86. Your socks must match your shoes.

87. You go swimming in your clothes.

88. You wear white socks with sandals.

89. You enjoy wearing the same outfit more than twice a week.

15

90. You're constantly reminding your children that twenty years ago you wore the same style clothes that they are wearing today.

YOu KnOw yOu're Still Ghetto If...

91. Your pillow has more makeup than your face did. (Wash your face before you go to bed.)

92. You take out your teeth to eat in front of people.

93. You have more than five uses for Q-Tips: ear cleaner, boogie remover, makeup applicator, nail-polish remover, electrical appliance cleaner.

94. You've ever slept in your panty hose.

95. Your collar has more makeup than your face.

96. You start flossing the week before going to the dentist.

97. You had your teeth removed and never bothered to replace them.

YOu KnOw yOu're Still Ghetto If...

98. You never smile 'cause you're missing a tooth. (Smile or get it fixed.)

99. You still wear Giorgio.

100. You get dressed to kill for work because you're going out later.

101. You shave your legs up to where your skirt stops.

102. You use pins in place of cuff links.

17

103. Your knees and elbows are always ashy.

104. You have a drawer full of makeup that's only been used once.

105. You have more gold in your mouth than Fort Knox.

106. You unbutton your shirt down to your navel.

Sharp As A Tack

107.   You save the old pieces of soap to make a new bar.

108.   You line your children up to bathe them with the same water.

18

YOu KnOw yOu're Still Ghetto If...

109. Your hairdo came from a seventies sitcom (e.g., Farrah Fawcett, Suzanne Somers, Diahann Carroll).

110. You wear a do-rag outside of your house.

111. You've worn wigs so long that even you think it's your own hair.

112. You take out your weave and tell people you got a haircut.

113. Your fingerwave needs to be redone and you just add more gel.

114. You've permed your hair so much that you don't know the natural texture of your hair.

YOu KNOw yOu're Still Ghetto If...

115. You are a man, you're going bald, and you have extensions or a jheri curl to hide the truth.

116. Anyone you know used a bowl to cut hair.

117. You have to bobby pin your hair back to make a ponytail.

118. You still have a flattop.

119. Your extensions are always falling out.

120. You dye your hair so much you look like Wayne Newton.

121. Your hair is so greasy you leave a stain on the pillow.

122. You grease your scalp.

Fried, Dyed, And Laid To The Side

YOu KNOW yOu're Still Ghetto If...

123. You've never been to the hairdresser and you brag about it.

124. Your dread breaks off and you sew it back.

Fried, Dyed, And Laid To The Side

YOu KnOw yOu're Still Ghetto If...

125. You shave your eyebrows off and draw them back on.

126. Your lipstick matches your clothes.

127. Your makeup sponge is crumbling.

128. You have more products in your bathroom than there are in the drugstore.

129. Your lipstick is darker than your skin color.

130. Your foundation is lighter than your skin color.

131. You still use bleaching cream (note: Ambi counts).

132. Your foundation looks like a chin strap.

YOu KNOw yOu're STill Ghetto If...

133. There is a white line down the middle of your nose to make it look smaller.

134. You use glitter for makeup.

135. Your rouge is applied in circles.

136. You think of Vaseline as makeup.

137. You refuse to buy makeup from companies who don't have models that look like you.

All Made Up And No Place To Go

YOu KnOW yOu're Still Ghetto If...

138. You're married to one of your ex's relatives.

139. Your children think that every man you dated is their uncle.

140. Your relatives are too removed to describe in one word (e.g., "my sister's cousin's uncle").

141. You refer to your gay relatives as being "that way" or "funny."

142. The back room of your house is like a nursing home.

143. You have a relative named NaNa, MeMa, or Big Mama but no one knows how they're related to you.

144. Everyone says that your uncle, who is in prison, is "away for a while."

145. You think your family is crazy but you're not.

YOu KnOW yOu're Still Ghetto If...

146. You have a crazy relative who has more sense than everybody else.

147. You have a baby sister named Baby Sis.

148. Everyone still calls you Little Ray because your father is Big Ray.

26

149. You give hard candy wrapped in tissue paper as Christmas presents.

150. When you eat nuts, you find it necessary to shake them in your hand first.

151. You have a cabinet full of half-used diet plans (e.g., Slimfast, Bahamian Diet, Nutrisystem, etc.).

152. You have soda and potato chips for breakfast.

153. You burn the toast and scrape off the black.

154. You eat Tums as candy.

155. You season everything with fatback but swear you don't know why your ankles are swollen.

Kiss It Up To God

156.
You serve
stale food.

YOu KNOW yOu're Still Ghetto If...

157. You eat more laxatives than vegetables.

158. You never drink water and brag about it.

159. You think you need to eat grease to live.

160. You can't drink something without shaking the glass.

161. You stir your drink with your finger.

29

162. You eat fish but you've never caught one.

163. You eat butter cookies with Kool-Aid.

164. You fish in the city. (Danger: expect to glow in the dark.)

165. You buy in bulk and never use it.

Kiss It Up To God

YOu KnOw yOu're Still Ghetto If...

166. Most of the food in cupboard came from your old house and the pancake mix is still taped shut.

167. You talk about what you're having for lunch while eating breakfast.

168. You always tell the story about never buying anything from a grocery store except salt.

Kiss It Up To God

YOu KNOW yOu're Still Ghetto If...

169. You keep flowers until they turn black.

170. You play the lottery more regularly than you pay your bills.

171. You never open your bills because you know what they're going to say.

172. Your trash can is always full and you smash it down with your feet.

173. You don't flush the toilet until morning to save water.

174. You can't understand what the big hoopla is over recycling because you never throw anything away.

Ghetto-Economics

YOu KnOW yOu're Still Ghetto If...

175. You think you exercised because you walked to the McDonald's.

176. You have every piece of exercise equipment sold on television, but you've never used any of them.

177. You wear bicycle pants but you've never ridden a bike.

178. Your treadmill is covered with clothes.

179. You wear workout clothing and never work out.

180. You consider getting up aerobic exercise.

181. Every time you sit down or get up, you go "whew."

182. You say you work out every day, but no one can tell the difference.

183. You have more NBA jerseys than professional players do.

YOu KnOW yOu're StIll Ghetto If...

184. You think of walking as a setback.

185. You watch aerobics tapes but never do them because the people are too skinny.

186. You won't exercise because your man says he likes some meat on his bones.

187. You wear weight lifting gloves to drive a car.

188. The only time you used your gym membership was the day you got it.

189. You have to open your pants when you eat.

190. You say you can't exercise because of medical reasons, and you've never been to the doctor.

Ghetto-Robics

yOu KnOw yOu're Still Ghetto If...

191. Every time someone mentions the word *diet*, you go into a comedy routine. ("I'm on a diet; I'm going to *die* if I don't get it." Or, "I'm on a seafood diet; I eat all the food I see.")

192. You think you had a great workout because you shouted in church.

193. You won't eat anybody's cooking.

194. You always eat before you go to a dinner party because "you never know what them people got."

Ghetto-Robics

YOu KNOW YOu're Still Ghetto If...

195. You talk on the phone while you're on the toilet.

196. You're constantly calling people to get somebody else's phone number.

197. You're watching the same TV program as everyone else but you're constantly asking questions about the program.

198. You talk back to the TV.

199. You need the TV on to fall asleep.

200. You sing along with TV commercials.

201. You become a human beat box in the middle of a conversation.

202. The first thing you read in the newspaper is the obituaries.

YOu KNOW yOu're Still Ghetto If...

203. You start every sentence with "we as black people."

204. You call someone's house and ask, "who's speaking?"

205. You see homeless people and you say, "they're probably rich."

38

206. You smoke so much you've mastered the art of flicking ashes.

207. You spit through your front teeth because you think it's cool.

208. You talk with your eyes closed.

209. You're always quoting motivational speakers.

210. You always include the 1 before giving long-distance numbers.

Things We *Still* Do

211.
All of your questions have two parts.

YOu KNOW yOu're Still Ghetto If...

212. You're at an open discussion and you have to give an autobiography before you ask a question.

213. You cook dinner in the wee hours of the morning.

214. You make your guests use your side door.

215. You go to someone's house but don't bring a present.

216. You visit someone and act like you live there.

217. You go out to dinner with friends and go to the bathroom when the check comes.

218. You try to figure out exactly what every person at dinner should owe. (Just divide it up.)

Things We *Still* Do

219. You lick your knife.

You Know You're Still Ghetto If...

220. You go on a road trip with friends and everyone suddenly falls asleep when you pull into the gas station.

221. You visit people, stay in their home, and talk about them after you leave.

222. You steal from the paperboy, grocery bagger, waitress, airport attendant, bellhop. (Yo! Tip those people!)

223. You kiss someone for the first time with your mouth wide open.

224. You tell people to page you, but never answer the page.

225. You always have a toothpick in your mouth.

226. After every meal, you suck your teeth in an attempt to clean them.

YOu KnOw yOu're Still Ghetto If...

227. You make people take off their shoes before they come in your home.

228. You won't allow anyone in your kitchen if they're wearing their coat and they just came in from outside.

Things We _Still_ Do

YOu KnOW yOu're Still Ghetto If...

229. You've never been to the other side of your town.

230. You have a strong opinion about something that you ain't never seen.

231. You think that everything you could ever want is right in your neighborhood.

232. You always try to get a discount from black-owned businesses.

233. You justify the use of the word *nigger* by saying there are black people and there are niggers.

234. You only eat from a restaurant where the cook is black. (Take that a step further.)

YOu KNOw yOu're Still Ghetto If...

235. You held the National Conference for Black Empowerment at the same place the NRA held theirs.

236. Every time you get together with friends you talk about what "the Man" has done. (Let's talk about what we can do.)

237. You think someone who is successful is no longer black.

238. You actually do think white women go better with a Brooks Brothers suit.

239. You're constantly doing things to prove that you're one of the good blacks.

240. You still use Kotex belts with pins.

241. All of your artwork has white people in it and you're black.

45.

Culture Shock

242.
You've
never
been to
the beach.

YOu KnOw yOu're Still Ghetto If...

243. You call yourself a cablasian. (Yes, we mean you, Tiger.)

244. You know everything your neighbors do.

245. Every time your children go away, you provide them with a list of relatives they've never met who just happen to live where they're going.

YOu KnOw yOu're Still Ghetto If...

Getting Over

246. You can hook up your own cable, turn back your gas meter, and add another phone extension, but you can't find a job.

247. All of your silverware came from a restaurant.

248. You buy or watch bootleg movies.

249. You add water to your whiskey so it can "go further."

250. You try to take food home from an all-you-can-eat buffet.

251. You smoke cigarettes but never buy them.

YOu KNOW yOu're Still Ghetto If...

252. You drink liquor but never buy it.

253. You join the record club ten times under ten different names.

254. You tape the bottom of your shoes because you intend on returning them.

255. You buy clothes for a special occasion and return them the next day.

256. You don't consider it stealing because you took it from "the Man."

257. You buy your clothes from the beauty parlor.

49

YOu KNOw yOu're Still Ghetto If...

Frontin'

258. The lining of your fur coat is torn.

259. Your watch doesn't work, but you keep wearing it for "sentimental reasons."

260. You tell people you're from someplace other than the little country town you're actually from.

261. You have a southern accent and ain't never been down south, or vice versa.

262. You brag about how tough your neighborhood is.

263. You tell people you have Indian blood, and that's why you have "good" hair. (There's no such thing as "good" hair, and yours is a perm.)

YOu KNOw yOu're Still Ghetto If...

264. You tell your coworkers about what your lover did to you last night.

265. When your beeper goes off, you look at it and say, "What does she want now?" loud enough for everybody to hear.

266. You talk on a cellular phone in a nightclub.

267. You brag about what you do in bed.

51

268. You are in your thirties and still brag about your high school days.

Frontin'

YOu KNOW yOu're STill Ghetto If...

269. You're still waiting for your forty acres and a mule. (I am.)

270. You go to the movies late and want the end (aisle) seat.

271. Someone in your family dies and you fight over their things. ("Mama said that was mine.")

272. You want your children to take care of you, but you didn't take care of them.

273. You're looking for a brother or sister who will pay your rent.

274. You really believe that the world owes you something.

YOu KnOw yOu're Still Ghetto If...

275. You still refer to Woolworth as the dime store.

276. Your family members don't know you by your real name.

277. You call someone at their house, but mispronounce their name.

278. You refer to items by their brand names (e.g., Kleenex, Sony Walkman, the Hoover).

279. You changed your name to make it sound "French" (e.g., Sharon, Tyron, Jackée).

280. You call your friends: Homey, Homes, Dog, My Brother, Ace Boon Coon, Money, Slim Slice, G, My Nigga, Girl, Boy, Dope, Black, Brotherman, Sistergirl.

Men Are From Up North, Women Are From Down South

281. You can't stand to hear about your wife/girlfriend's menstrual period and you've been together 50-11 years.

282. You take all of your dates to the movies.

283. You haven't been on a date since you got married.

284. You're looking for your "other half." (Complete yourself.)

285. You take all your dates to your favorite spot.

286. You don't take your dates to your favorite spot. (Ghetto if you do, ghetto if you don't.)

287. You think all men are dogs.

288. You think all women are gold diggers.

YOu KnOw yOu're Still Ghetto If...

289. You're looking for a woman who's just like your moms.

290. You and your significant other have foods for nicknames (e.g., peach cobbler, strawberry shortcake, honey, pudding).

Ghetto Love

291. All your ex-boyfriends look alike.

292. You keep a picture of your ex in your wallet.

293. You sing in a woman's ear when you slow dance.

294. You're always talking about your exes to whoever you are currently involved with.

295. You break up with somebody and then try to get back the presents you bought them.

YOu KNOw yOu're Still Ghetto If...

296. You've been dating someone for more than a month, but you've never met their family or friends.

297. You look at your girlfriend's mother to see how she'll look when she's older.

298. You watch how a man treats his mother to see how he'll treat you.

YOu KNOW yOu're Still Ghetto If...

299. Girl, I'll drink your bathwater.

300. You so pretty, you could've been twins.

301. I want to know you. Hell, my mama wants to know you.

302. If loving you is wrong, I ain't never gonna be right.

303. Do fries go with that shake?

304. All that meat and no potatoes.

305. Come on, baby, let me rock your world.

306. We can make some pretty babies.

YOu KNOW yOu're Still Ghetto If...

307. You lick your finger and stick it in someone's ear, and actually think that you've turned them on. (Note: That's not sexy, it's nasty.)

308. Ain't nothing a skinny woman can do, but show me where the big ones are.

309. Nothing likes a bone but a dog.

310. More cushion, less pushin'.

311. You must be a descendant of the Hottentots.

312. Anything more than a mouthful is a waste.

Ghetto Superstitions

313. You put your purse on the floor, and you'll always be broke.

314. You flush or burn your hair so a bird doesn't eat it and give you a headache.

315. You spill salt and throw it over your shoulder because you think you'll have bad luck.

316. Someone steps over you and you think you won't grow.

317. Your left hand itches and you think you're going to get a letter.

318. Your right hand itches and you think you'll get money.

319.
Your foot
itches and
you think
you're
going on
a trip.

YOu KnOW yOu're Still Ghetto If...

320. Your nose itches and you think someone's coming to visit. (Note: If any of the above are happening to you, go bathe.)

321. Your left eye jumps and you expect trouble.

322. Your right eye jumps and you expect good news.

323. A bird flies into your house and you think someone is going to die.

324. You think death comes in threes. (It comes in the thousands.)

325. You dream that somebody died and so you know that someone must be pregnant.

326. You think a widow's peak means you're wise.

Ghetto Superstitions

YOu KNOW yOu're Still Ghetto If...

327. A child is born with a veil over their head (after-birth) and you think they must be psychic.

328. A child is born breech, and everybody says, "Trouble coming into the world, they'll be trouble going out."

329. You think you can tell what color a child will be by the tip of their ears or the color of their fingernails.

330. You think a child will visit because someone dropped a spoon.

331. You think a woman will visit because someone dropped a fork.

332. You think a man will visit because someone dropped a knife.

333. It's bad luck to put your hat on the bed.

Ghetto Superstitions

334. You can't move into a new house before it's been prayed over.

335. You think it's bad luck to visit a new house without taking a present.

64

YOu KnOw yOu're Still Ghetto If...

336. You don't know shit from shinola.

337. If I do, Skippy got hair on his teeth.

338. You ain't got a pot to piss in or a window to throw it out.

339. I been working from can't see to can't see.

340. You thought like Lit. Lit thought he farted but he really shit.

341. He's just breath and britches.

342. All he's got is his hat and that.

343. I'll slap the black off of you.

344.
I'll slap the taste out of your mouth.

YOu KnOw yOu're Still Ghetto If...

345. I'll knock you from amazing grace to a floating opportunity.

346. If you touch me, you'll draw back a nub.

347. If you see a boy, smack him.

348. I brought you into this world; I'll take you out.

349. Ain't no telling.

350. The apple don't fall far from the tree.

351. Same ol', same ol'. (Nothing has changed.)

352. Lie down with dogs, you get up with fleas.

353. If you cut somebody's legs off, you won't grow. (Talking others down doesn't make you bigger.)

354.
Whatever
floats
your
boat.

YOu KnOw yOu're Still Ghetto If...

355. If you lie, you'll steal.

356. Pretty is as pretty does.

357. The law is for the lawless.

358. Bes that way sometimes.

359. I'm gonna open up a can of whip-ass on you.

360. I know dat's right.

361. Nothin' from nothin'.

362. True dat.

363. Right, right.

364. I heard that.

365.
You want some of this.

YOu KNOw yOu're Still Ghetto If...

366. I'll put my foot so far up your ass, you'll taste shoe polish.

367. Stepped on a pin, the pin bent, that's the way the story went. (It's over and done with.)

368. If I'm lyin', I'm flyin'.

369. Signifying is worse than stealing.

370. If you're light, you're all right; brown, stick around; black, get back.

371. Lord willing and the creek don't rise.

372. The blacker the berry, the sweeter the juice, but when it's that black it ain't no use.

373. The empty barrel makes the most noise.

YOu KNOW yOu're Still Ghetto If...

374. When it rains, it pours.

375. There's no fool like an old fool.

YOu KnOw yOu're Still Ghetto If...

376. You read the back of everything.

377. You keep newspaper clippings so long you can't remember what they pertained to.

378. You've seen every new movie, but haven't read a book.

379. You turn in an assignment with stains on it.

380. Your homework is ripped out of a spiral notebook.

I Read It In *Jet*

YOu KnOw yOu're Still Ghetto If...

381. The only book you have is the Bible, and you don't ever read it.

382. You get your nails done more often than you read the paper.

383. You're more proud of the texture of your child's hair than your are of what's in their head.

384. You read the cereal box at breakfast.

385. You have more videos than books.

386. You start your conversations by talking about who died.

387. You see soap operas as a form of therapy.

388. You get all your news from *Jet* magazine.

I Read It In *Jet*

YOu KNOW yOu're Still Ghetto If...

389. Your three-year-old can operate the VCR.

390. You use so much medicine, your four-year-old can bring you the exact one you need.

391. Your underage children earn more than you do.

392. You suspect that your child is doing something illegal but you don't do anything about it because the money is good.

393. You take your babies to R-rated movies.

394. Your child has more white dolls than black, and she's not white.

395. You go fishing but never take your children.

YOu KnOw yOu're Still Ghetto If...

396. Your children have never played jacks or marbles.

397. You comb your children's hair on your front step.

398. Your twelve-year-old has had her eyebrows plucked.

399. You're always telling your children about how bad you had it when you were young.

400. Your children are not allowed to go in anybody else's home without your approval.

YOu KNOw yOu're Still Ghetto If...

401. You describe people by how dark or light they are.

402. You still think that hair can be good or bad. (Yeah, I know it was in the last book, but I needed to say it again.)

403. You describe people using any of the following: hainty, high yella, redbone, blue black, coffee, café au lait, smooth black, so black he's purple, almond, brown skint, light skint.

404. You brag about being everything except black.

405. You stay out of the sun because you don't want to get blacker.

YOu KnOw yOu're Still Ghetto If...

Pass The Plate: Ghetto Churches

406. Your church is always doing building fund-raisers, but they still haven't built anything.

407. You pay more in church assessments than you give to the poor.

408. Every man who joins the church thinks he's been called into the ministry, just because he's a man.

409. A new man comes to church and everybody's trying to date him before he can even get to the altar.

410. Your pastor preaches for an hour and a half and only reads one scripture.

411. Your pastor preaches for an hour and a half.

YOu KnOW yOu're Still Ghetto If...

412. You tell people "the preacher really preached" but you can't remember the sermon.

413. A young woman gets pregnant and she's not allowed to sing in the choir, but the man who impregnated her is.

414. The offering time is really a fashion show in disguise.

415. You have church service every night of the week. (Get out of your church and get into the world.)

416. The church is the nicest thing on the block and you brag about it.

417. One person gets all of the choir's solos. (See *The Preacher's Wife*.)

418. You leave every service early to go eat.

Pass The Plate: Ghetto Churches

YOu KnOw YOu're Still Ghetto If...

419. You're constantly looking for a new church because the folks in the one you left were full of sin. (Check yourself.)

420. You think that anything that goes wrong is because of the devil. (Note: You had a hand in it.)

421. There's more drama in your church than in a soap opera.

422. Your church single group spends all of its time trying to get married. (Note: Use your single time to serve.)

423. The white-gloved "ursher" is always standing by with a glass of cold orange juice as soon as the pastor finishes his sermon.

424. Your relatives don't like to be around you because you're so holy.

425. The pastor puts on a cape when he finishes his sermon.

YOu KNOW YOu're Still Ghetto If...

426. The fund-raiser thermometer in the church lobby never moves.

427. Every time a new man joins the congregation, you swear he's the one because he's the one the Lord showed you in a dream.

428. All of your church dresses have sequins.

429. Your pastor has to change clothes immediately after he preaches.

430. The offering extends to the lobby.

431. Your church is held in a building other than the church.

432. Your pastor has another job.

Pass The Plate: Ghetto Churches

YOu KnOW yOu're Still Ghetto If...

433. The bride and groom's vows rhyme.

434. The groom has a top hat and cane.

435. It's an Afrocentric wedding and everyone has a perm.

436. It's an Afrocentric wedding with a Eurocentric structure.

437. No one knows which side to sit on.

438. The bride and groom jump the broom.

Ghetto-Nuptials

That's *My* Song

439. Your conversations about music always come back to Aretha's clothes.

440. All your tapes are copied.

441. You've ever been to a Parliament concert.

442. You graduated from the "old school."

443. You put on a record and declare, "y'all don't know nothin' 'bout this."

444. The majority of your music collection is on vinyl.

445. You can't listen to Al Green without talking back.

446.
You realize that Nina Simone is an icon.

YOu KNOW yOu're Still Ghetto If...

447. You suck your teeth before 10 A.M.

448. You feed people according to their size.

449. You wear leather in the islands.

450. You get dressed up (ruffles and cummerbund) to fly.

451. Your neighborhood has its own drunk.

452. You live on an island and can't swim.

453. You chew and eat your bones.

454. You walk like you're in a parade.

455.
You eat three starches in one meal.

YOu KnOW yOu're Still Ghetto If...

456. You're at a party and you hear "buoy! buoy!" and you know what it means.

457. You drink Maubi, Sorrel, Sea Moss, Gingerbeer, Malta, Ovaltine, Guinness.

458. You drink stout as a backbone tonic.

459. You need a washout (bush tea).

460. You go to a wedding just for the black cake.

461. Your boyfriend/husband has two other girlfriends and no one seems to mind.

462. You only go to church on Easter for the bun and cheese.

463. You drop your h's or pronounce h's where they're not supposed to be. (Pronounce your haitches you h'ignorant h'ass.)

West Indian Ghetto

YOu KNOw yOu're Still Ghetto If...

464. You think you're not country anymore because you live in New York City.

465. You're a grown man and you go to a high school to pick up girls.

466. You bathe in the sea.

467. You go to the bathroom in the bush.

468. You wash your underwear at night.

469. You live by the 11th commandment, "Never miss a freebs." (Something that is free.)

470. The groom's family has to go to the bride's house to propose.

West Indian Ghetto

YOu KnOw yOu're Still Ghetto If...

Ghetto Dances

471. the Slop

472. the Grind

473. Hand Dancing

474. Steppin'

475. the Bop

476. the Electric Slide

477. the Percolator

478. the Tootsie Roll

479. the Penguin

YOu KnOw yOu're Still Ghetto If...

480. the Bus Stop

481. the Butterfly

Ghetto Dances

YOu KnOW yOu're Still Ghetto If...

482. You still have rope burns around your back from double Dutch.

483. You make more noise playing dominoes than you do when you make love.

484. Anytime you get together with friends, you break out into a game of spades.

485. You tied your jump rope to a doorknob and jumped by yourself.

YOu KnOw yOu're Still Ghetto If...

486. You spend more time with your car than the people who ride in it.

487. You care more about the fresh air in your car than in your lungs.

488. You have a necklace with a Mercedes symbol but you drive a Pinto.

489. There's an air freshener with a Playboy symbol hanging from your rearview mirror.

Ghetto Wheels

YOu KnOW yOu're Still Ghetto If...

490. You refer to your BMW as a ho catcher.

491. Your car has a spoiler that's a different color than the car.

492. You made your own sunroof.

493. Your car seat covers have your initials on them.

94

494. You have an aquarium but no fish.

495. All your fish died from ich.

496. You think you should share your pet snake with the neighborhood.

497. Your dog answers to the name "here boy."

498. You have a dog named "Dog" and a cat named "Cat."

499. Your dog belongs to the neighborhood.

Ghetto Pets

YOu KNOW YOu're Still Ghetto If...

500. You take your own meals on an airplane trip.

501. You recycle your chewing gum.

502. When you do laundry, you have to find change in the sofa.

503. You give old Christmas gifts to someone else.

504. You leave change around your house for hard times.

505. You give your children an allowance, and then later have to borrow it back.

506. You check pay phones for change.

507. You look for change in other people's sofas.

You Know you're Still Ghetto If...

Ghetto Comebacks

508. *Hey honey child:*
I'm not your honey. I'm not your child; I'm just a friend to make you smile.

509. *Mind your business:*
My mind is my business.

510. *Shut up!*
Shut don't go up, price do, take my advice and shut up too.

511. *What?*
Chicken butt. Go 'round the corner and lick it up. I eat the chicken, you eat the gut.

512. *You can kiss what I twist and I don't mean my wrist.*

YOu KnOw yOu're Still Ghetto If...

513. *Mother F——:*
Did you see my shoe under your mama's bed last night?

514. *Who did that?*
First one who said it, let it.
First one who smelt it, dealt it.

YOu KNOW YOu're Still Ghetto If...

515. You think of fashion shows as a cultural event.

516. There is an announcer who describes every detail.

517. The announcer finishes each description by saying, "You go, girl!"

518. All of the clothes came from local department stores.

519. The fashion show lasts for at least three hours.

520. There's more people in the show than in the audience.

521. The models come back and forth more than twice, in the same outfit.

522. The music tape is constantly being re-cued.

YOu KNOW yOu're Still Ghetto If...

523. The clothes are new but the shoes are old.

524. The hair styles look like wedding cakes.

525. Someone slips and falls, and everybody says, "That' all right."

526. There's a lingerie segment.

527. Everyone is wearing sunglasses.

528. All the clothes were made by the models.

Fashion Shows

YOu KnOW yOu're Still Ghetto If...

529. You have a pair of house shoes under your desk.

530. You call in sick on the Friday before every holiday.

531. The cafeteria at work always smells like whatever you had for dinner the night before.

532. You're always buying stuff from the vending machine at work but you never have your own money.

533. You tell your boss all of your business.

534. You blast your radio at work, and sing even louder when your song comes on.

535. You use the bathroom at work like you would if you were at home.

YOu KnOw yOu're Still Ghetto If...

536. You have a desk full of snack food.

537. Your coworkers can tell when you've been eating Funyuns.

104

YOu KNOW yOu're StilI Ghetto If...

538. You have a candy dish, but no candy.

539. Your children have to blow on their Nintendo to make it work.

540. You're always carrying a bottle of water, but you never drink any.

541. Your socks smell like Doritos.

542. You tell people, "I could lose weight if I wanted to."

543. There are crumbs in your bed.

544. All of your furniture has little water rings on it.

545. You yell at everybody else's kids and yours terrorize the neighborhood.

546.
You had to come home when the streetlights came on.

YOu KNOW yOu're Still Ghetto If...

547. As soon as you get home from church, you're on the phone gossiping.

548. You had to sleep four to a bed.

549. You had to share a bike with your baby brother.

550. You had a fish tank, but no fish.

551. You've seen a celebrity, and you tell everyone that you know them.

552. All the pictures on your walls are crooked.

553. Your TV doesn't work, but you keep it anyway.

554. Your favorite comedian is Rudy Ray Moore.

555. Your car always needs a jump, and you don't own cables.

Ghetto Afterthought

556.
Everything in your house matches.

YOu KNOW yOu're Still Ghetto If...

557. Your wedding colors were maroon and gold.

558. The police know your address by heart.

559. Your children write on your walls, but not in their books.

560. None of your CDs are in the right case.

Ghetto Afterthought

YOu KnOw yOu're Still Ghetto If...

As I mentioned in the introduction, which I'm sure that you've read, the purpose of this test is to determine which of our ghetto ways we should get rid of and which we should keep. By now you have already realized what some of these items are. Go back over the contents of the book, and discuss with family and friends which of these things can be beneficial to ourselves and to our community, and which of them are detrimental.

Items that are in **boldface** are items that should be kept. There are others that are not so obvious. Because this is about your healing, it is up to you to figure out which they are.

Don't take yourself or this test too seriously. Enjoy.